Axe in Hand

Axe in Hand

Melanie Moro-Huber

The New York Quarterly Foundation, Inc.
New York, New York

NYQ Books™ is an imprint of The New York Quarterly Foundation, Inc.

The New York Quarterly Foundation, Inc.
P. O. Box 2015
Old Chelsea Station
New York, NY 10113

www.nyqbooks.org

Copyright © 2012 by Melanie Moro-Huber

All rights reserved. No part of this book may be used or reproduced in any manner whatsoever without written permission of the author except in the case of brief quotations embodied in critical articles and reviews.

First Edition

Set in New Baskerville

Layout and Design by Raymond P. Hammond
Cover Photo: "West Rosebud Chopping Block" by Sherry O'Keefe
http://toomuchaugust.wordpress.com

Library of Congress Control Number: 2011942032

ISBN: 978-1-935520-56-6

Axe in Hand

Acknowledgments

"Feathers and Flute," *Opus 40*; "The Bookbinding Lesson," "Ice Storm," "Freak Show1,2,3 and 5," "Glossing," "Lunar Navigator," "Origami Boat Race," "Subtraction," "Free Falls," "Navigating the Air," "Star City Coffin Club," "Paper Philosophy," "Come sun up," and "Habeas Corpus," *Ahadada Reader 3*; "When," "So," *New York Quarterly*.

"Born on a Blue Day," "I think God wears shoes," "The Year of the Stinkbug" were published by Connotation Press, June 2011.

"Troublesome Creek '93" won the 2010 Golden Nib award for poetry, Roanoke Chapter of the Virginia Writers Association, third place in state.

Special thanks to Amy Glynn Greacen for going over the manuscript with acute attention to detail, Mara Eve Robbins for reading the manuscript more times than should be asked of a person, Mei Li Inouye for convincing me to run away and re-gather my writing after the hard-drive crash, Jeanne Larsen for running down sources, Richard Dillard and Claudia Emerson for being gracious mentors, Raymond Hammond, of course, for putting up with the million tweaks, and most of all my family, those here and gone and far away, the kids for letting me sleep in and my husband, Lee for understanding and patience above and beyond, the kindness in the way he said "good night" and "good morning" as he put up with the days I went without sleeping, ignoring him and everything else around me.

How cut haft for an axe?

*Who hacks
holds a haft…*

*To hack an axe-haft an axe
hacks;*

the pattern's near.

—from *The Book of Songs* (Shih Ching)
Ezra Pound (1875-1972), translator

Contents

Dragonfly Evacuee / *13*
Habeas Corpus (Pencil People) / *14*
Toilet Paper / *15*
Glossing / *16*
Origami Boat Race / *17*
Agnostic Relationship / *18*
Rock Paper Scissors / *19*
Eating an Artichoke / *20*
Feathers and Flute / *21*
Lights On in "Hell-fer-Sartin" / *23*
Freak Show 1: Tesla's Pigeon Wife / *24*
Pogo Moose, Fairbanks, Alaska, December 2007 / *25*
Murmurations / *26*
Sorting it Out / *27*
Freak Show 2: Masterpiece Theatre / *28*
Freak Show 3: Fanny Mill's Wish / *29*
Once we gathered oysters while children played / *30*
when? / *31*
Dig In / *32*
Troublesome Creek '93 / *33*
Harper Lee / *34*
Come sun up. / *35*
Loom / *36*
Make Believe / *37*
Paper Philosophy / *38*
How Many Poets Does it Take to Change a Light-bulb? / *39*
Concrete / *40*
A Question About What's Essential / *41*
Opus 40 / *42*
Tankas to Float Down the River for Mara's 40th Birthday / *43*
City on the Sea / *44*
The Doll Head Stories / *46*
At the Outline of Night / *47*
Treading Consciousness / *48*
Whence Came Thou—Watermelon / *49*
Frames, unhinged / *50*
Time to Go (a ballad) / *51*

Free Falls   /   *53*
Cosmic Constructions   /   *55*
The Cowboy's Rain-dance   /   *56*
So   /   *57*
The Imp of the Perverse (revisited)   /   *59*
Star City Coffin Club   /   *61*
The Year of the Stink Bug   /   *62*
I think that God wears shoes   /   *64*
What sometimes you find   /   *65*
Freak Show 4: Gone Rogue   /   *66*
Ice Storm   /   *67*
My Children Picked the Berries from the Hollytree   /   *68*
The Bookbinding Lesson   /   *69*
What we carry home   /   *70*
Surprise Epilogue at Dawn   /   *72*
Lunar Navigator   /   *73*
Luminosity: Radiant energy and other forms   /   *74*
Dad's Tomatoes   /   *75*
Graveyard   /   *77*
Look up   /   *78*
Gifts of Faith (Without Conviction)   /   *79*
Energy Efficient   /   *80*
Born on a Blue Day (Daniel Tammet)   /   *81*
Aiken's Still Makin' Music   /   *82*
Freak Show 5: There have been dancing plagues before.   /   *83*
Preservation   /   *84*
Attrition   /   *85*
Subtraction   /   *86*
Only the Air   /   *87*
She fell asleep before the execution   /   *89*
After Dreaming of Tornados   /   *90*
Mosaic   /   *91*
Unearthed   /   *92*
Axe in Hand (The Perpetually Present State of Poetry)   /   *93*

Axe in Hand

Dragonfly Evacuee

There is comfort in being the same as everyone else.
A fly among houseflies, gathered together in daily rituals.
The rubbing together of legs, a ceremony, or just keeping warm?
I haven't figured it out yet. And then there's always
the latest buzz about disturbing, yet titillating, sightings
of fly swatters.

Of course, everyone pretends not to notice my odd color,
more green than black, not to mention my long thin
iridescent wings, four instead of two.

Several times I've been asked:
"Where do *you* come from?" I just smile vaguely
and describe some unimpressive garbage can.

I'm beginning to wonder how much longer
they're going to buy this.

For one thing, I can't stand looking at the world upside down.
It makes me dizzy. And even though I enjoy the whole
rubbing legs routine, when I hear about how quickly
maggots grow in a day, I start to twitch.

Still I'm starting to believe walls are happy enough places.
Yet I must confess when the air is warm I slip outside
to visit the river, and when I hear a frog calling for a mate,
or see the cattails dipping down, the water-skippers playing
hop-scotch, I think about water for a long, long time.
How generous. How disengaged.

Habeas Corpus (Pencil People)

(Based on artwork by Nadine Jarvis)

Ash from one human body
can produce 240 pencils.

Cedar tree coffin, cedar tree
pencil, the line will hold the weight of the hand,
but the hand itself holds nothing.

Any body can be used, but which word
will restore a life? Sharpen the head,
hair, teeth and elbows,

to know (gnosis), to write:
(graphite) the difference between (penna)
the feather pen, and pencillus, (little tail)
the pencil.

That which is paper is corporate, is skin,
is corporeal in the mind of a kind of company.

Ash from one human body can produce

an empty palm, the flesh becomes
the Word in the company of leftover shavings,
the word saved in a box,

a lifetime supply.

Toilet Paper

An ocean of trees died
just so I could wipe my ass today.
Did I think about them, wonder what cure
for cancer, aids, pimples, was lost forever
under the wealth of their canopy.

Nope.

Did I stop to appreciate the complex
molecular structure
of delicate carbon strands, poetic
in their determination to exist
as pristine white fiber,
cushy, yet surprisingly strong?

Nope.

It was only much later while looking
at this blank face of open space
that I began to wonder about
the genealogy of paper, roots,
leaves, earth, sky, rain,

falling just the way it did
when the first volcanic eruption
condensed into a cloud.

Did you know water recycles itself,
and we drink from the same well the first
fuzzy men and dinosaurs drank from?

The culmination of a million years evolution:
$E=mc2$, e-mail, facebook, organ transplants,
joules of light dotting the earth
like the copycat stars they are,

all reduced to this:
thin white paper, falling apart,
swirling down a funnel of water.

Glossing

Have you not seen the faces in the wood?
He asks, pointing to oak veneered panels.

Are they old? Where do they come from?
I don't see anything, but I smell a cadence
of sandalwood, a vanilla cigarette, mimosa.
We dance, drunkenly,
in front of plastic logs in a gas fire.

Even a cotton ball can kill you. He teases,
pulling away at the fibers, smudging white
between his thumb and forefinger.

How? I contend, there are some things
that exist that can never be used as weapons.

He laughs. Silly girl, this house has marinated
for so long in the sounds of the flesh
once we are gone, once we are gone
our vanishing bodies will emboss the wall.

Origami Boat Race

They didn't hold shape long.

Since neither was made of wood
and plastic was never quite pliable enough
those fingers that forced the folds
shoved them off.

They took on water—80%
more or less. A river rafting trip
gone wrong.

Recovery is a bloated business
in all this sinking
because no one sails well on paper
and we are not the masters of currents.

If there were tour guides,
they'd just lie.

Even an amoeba knows this
but keeps faith
in the absurd joy of osmosis,
fragile boats riding the gutter rapids

so much drowning in tablespoons.

Agnostic Relationship

Oh
He's quiet now.
That's all I know.
Words condense, evaporate
Leave a residue.

I can't tell if the silence
Is an empty well or a leaf
Adrift on an ocean.

I don't understand
This surface stillness
What he won't say and why.

I don't know how to find
The hushing places, where I hear
The fallen float, voiceless, and yet
They sing.

Rock Paper Scissors

She sells seashells at the seashow-ah. Seashells at the seashow-ah. Seashow-arr, seashowerr...

My daughter has the "s" sound down
but she still hasn't quite got her "r's" so she practices
as she cuts snowflakes to hang on the windows,
keeps all the scraps and glues them into ice-paper sculptures.

"What is today again?" She asks for the third time.
"What time will you be home?
How many minutes?"

The answer is never soon enough, and I wish I could tell her
it doesn't matter if there is no ocean, no shore,
she can still spend her day looking for sea glass,
or imagining that bottle,
the one tossed from a ship while the ship was taking on water,
or if it helps, think about the message inside,
a secret note, not so secret really because bottles
tossed in oceans always say the same thing:

I love you. I'll miss you. See you again someday.

Instead I tell her about what I found
in the trash—sheet music *Fur Elise,*
I saved it to quarter the pages and weave
some words among the half and whole notes.

And this is how we save a ship, make a big thing small,
fold it over, put in a bottle or a pocket, carry it with us
wherever we go.

Can we, can we really?

No. But I will not mention regret,
the one thing I do believe, rock heart paper weights
keep the wind from blowing
all of us away.

Eating an Artichoke

There is no basket of bread
and fish substitute.
No matter how steady the hand holding
the whole green globe or northern star,
when you cut the thistle from the fleshy bracts,
cleave the whole into halves,
the parts are always uneven
and the water changes color when it's done.
So you pry away the petals, note the irony,
how the sunchoke is a tuber which grows
underground and changed its name to Jerusalem.
Know it is work, nothing but
scraping the inedible from the center
to expose the most tender,
but save this part for last;
there is so much more in this to savor.

Feathers and Flute

Below the plume there is the down,
and how else would a white dove
become a phoenix but stitched within
an ivory refuge for the heated brain?
A thin spine makes a better headrest.
A quill, however, knows no mercy.

Softness requires a certain amount of power,
a reverence for nesting. Or some would say
a precise amount of time before
the body conforms to the pillow.
The impression, though slight, endures.
I discovered this once, in the temple,
when the air started to give
a spike of white came whiffling
down to the prayer altar.

It wasn't my temple,
and it wasn't my prayer,
but I bowed my head anyway and said yes.

~~~~

I hear there is a darkly-carved cavern
where winged fossils fill the walls
and oscillations of the night sky
do not matter if you enter here.
I followed dusk's trail to the uneven tracks
of dawn, but there was no one there, no cave,
just a crystal surface of scales
above an empty arroyo.
Sometimes it is too much to take in.

~~~~

*Once the road was icy and cold, a woman lost control
(did they find her?) Light as a feather
stiff as a board, light as*

~~~~

My fingers stagger across those scales
all along the reptile's twisted spine.
*You can taste the bitterness in the air
and consume yourself if need be.*
He trembles and tells me,
cast aside this paper skin.
He is as dreadful as Quetzalcoatl,
and dance in your bones,
but soft, so much softer than I thought.

Lights On in "Hell-fer-Sartin"

'Round Troublesome Creek all the hills have names
and that one's Hell-fer-Sartin. The south-side's cut
like a cake, stone sliced into a giant stairway
that starts at the rip-rap by the road and steps
right on up to the sky.

Power poles run from the cliffs of Hell
for certain to each hill and house up the holler.
The men run lines like spun web.

"Light bulbs 'tain't that great aftern' all," the women say.
It was easier to overlook the coal dust in the dimmer
light of a lamp. Now they've moved everything inside
outside and are "beatin' evra-damn thang" with brooms.

And just this morning at the bottom of Hell-fer-Sartin
there was a man with long black hair and feathers
playing a flute and burning some type of grass. The smoke
cleared the mountain easy, without so much as a breeze.

Freak Show 1: Tesla's Pigeon Wife

The wind blew all night. This morning it is still
indiscriminately shredding limbs and knocking wind-
chimes down. There is no logic to what we love.

At first, the lure was a bread crumb trail
she followed to his window, where with peculiar
and solemn awe he watched her coo. The gentle swell
of her white throat transformed him. The sound
made everything conductively clear to him, if he could
just divide it all by three—the ledge, feathers and flight,
the wind, coils and alternating currents. The spin
of the earth, the soil, and gravity. He'd build a tower
for her, a tower which would charge the air
with limbs of electricity reaching out
across the night sky to the filament inside of glass,
a hushed glow three miles in the distance.
Then he sang,

so softly she was coaxed inside. He named her
his muse. She spent the rest of her days
pillowed in a metal cage. When she was gone
he made an altar from her dainty bones.
Nothing made sense again.

Pogo Moose, Fairbanks, Alaska, December 2007

The men are running lines again,
new power cables, strung on the ground in the arctic,
miles and miles across that tundra.
Tundra, oh my, such tundra!

They start to pull and—lift off!
A 60-inch bull tangles in the wire, antlers
and wacky legs all a-dangle above the pines,
the moose forced up close and personal with the sky.

Did he think thoughts, I wonder
that a ground-bound moose never could have?
Some say new heights can bring new clarity,
a spark in the brain crossing the evolutionary divide.

Or say a stepping stone, strobe lights
of awareness that will blast off forever and ever
from behind those moose-eyes. And from now on
all his progeny (calf-brains) will be wired to know
what it means to be airborne. I imagine,

if such is the case, there most certainly will be
flying Bullwinkles in our future. Someday,
someday, unless he just drops down to earth,
still alive, maybe more alive now, but peeved,

already agitated because it is rutting season after all.
Unharmed, mostly unaffected, he had better things to do
than evolve. Into the forest he bounds, to pogo
on and on, he learned this much of (dare I say it)

the language of fowl. What music? Lust hangs
all, so chalk the stumbling up to vertigo, is there
nothing else?

Murmurations

They are not natives, these usurpers of cardinals,
these black cloakers of trees. True, they are perfectly rude,
the way they swathe tree limbs in shit and startle the atmosphere
with their twerping, which is of no particular melody,
and even by bird standards they're probably considered
very ugly. Starlings—they just can't keep it together.

I don't know if they navigate along obscure magnetic lines, or by
a common twitch in each individual skull, or from the singular
wave of sound from the hum of a million wings,
I wonder as they speckle the sky, criss-crossing eastward
always east, where the light began.

Sorting it Out

I can't recall when I first began the ritual of forgetting. Somewhere between the car and the front door I have already forgotten them. I don't think of them again until my husband asks me where they are. I search the usual places. Kitchen table. Fireplace mantle. Dresser. Hallway. No, no, no and no. There's got to be a flash of silver somewhere. Socks and earrings do this to me too. My husband panics and says, "I can't believe you did this to me again! How can a person go from one room to the next holding something right in their hands and not know where they put it?" I don't know. "Reality is a tricky thing," I say. He doesn't buy it. I don't blame him. He always knows where things are. His lunch box goes next to the fridge (which thankfully never moves). His wallet goes inside his ball-cap which is on top of the lunch box, next to the fridge. He places the credit cards in the wallet in a particular order. His shoes are on the right side of the bed. His keys are on the second hook in the hallway. He has a box in his closet called the "Dad box" where he has saved all the first hair-cuts, first lost teeth, first baby booties. He actually likes sorting socks. I appreciate this ability but his way baffles me. Not that he puts everything back in the same place but that he knows how to remember. He remembers the Kroger's card goes in front of the debit card, and the debit card goes behind the Citibank card, and the Citibank card goes, well, I don't know. I've already lost the Kroger card and the Debit card and I assume this is why my husband panics. There are holes in his wallet that make him uneasy. "I'm not giving you the debit card ever again." He tells me for the tenth or eleventh or hundredth time. What I'm trying to get at here is structure, the opposite of chaos, the reverse of entropy. I begin a poem in my mind as I search. It starts like this: *Somewhere between the car and the front door.* But it flies away, somewhere else, and now it's gone too, and I think I keep forgetting because I'm teaching myself to accept loss. And when I really accept that whatever it is—is gone—just gone, being lost does not feel like the worst thing. I let it go, and forget again. Always in this moment, in the second forgetting, the letting go part of me remembers and whispers to the part of me which doesn't. There, underneath the pile of newspapers, on the table all along.

Freak Show 2: Masterpiece Theatre

They put the powdered parts of him
in Starbucks cups, then salt and peppered him
on the ground. The rest of him, not stolen, endures.

Perhaps the answer will be found
in the riddled hollows of Alistar Cooke's bones.
But it doesn't really matter if he became a relic

or just a gruesome ornament adorning the mantel.

Freak Show 3: Fanny Mill's Wish

Her feet were laced into pillowcases
and three goat skins hemmed together,
but it didn't make walking any easier.
Fanny Mill was as modest as she was famous.
Her hemlines were nearly invisible
and her stitches the smallest in the county.
She should have been a seamstress;
instead, for ten cents she'd lift her skirts
past her knees and endure the bulging
bull-frog eyes. The cavernous mouths,
always open, always the un-hinged red tongues.
Children were the worst.
They asked questions.

Big Foot Ohio Girl
Her gaze would fix itself to the wall and her shoulders
and arms, all angles and squares, would slope
lower each year. Finally her wrists settled
to her lap as her boney fingers formed a pyramid
over her womb.

She did not know when she stopped imagining
the unattainable—running, socks, real socks
made of wool, a graceful step, and a man
who could love her and not button up shoes.

Once we gathered oysters while children played

Near a toppled lighthouse, among the markers of the fallen,
Forgotten stones. This at least will not be lost to sea.
The wind bucks against my shoulders and now I'm stuck
Looting dunes and tide pools, sifting—
Seaweed, driftwood, sand-dollars, starfish.
Once we pried open shells and sliced our fingers,
But I can't recall the pain, just the taste—mouths
Overwhelmed, loving the layers, the salt waves, the deep
Pacific we set free on our tongues.

when?

there is a lift in a time that happens at sunrise
a moment when even the bees are still
before the hive starts to hum and the noise of color
calls loudly from among quiet spaces of green
and the mist that rolls around the mountains all night
traces the river down to the valley
like curious fingers trailing the spine
of some sleeping form.
it is always at this time that you come
inside my stillness as I watch
the sun slip strange shadows across your face
and each day, until that day that I am
rocking on my porch,
or hushing the flowers with water,
the quiet will die a little.
I'll hear your skin touch mine,
or maybe just the wind rustling sheets on the line,
and I'll suck in that sound until my lungs ache,
until the quiet slips through me,
until my body shines with a soft hum
like a tuning fork
you hold close enough to your ear.

Dig In

It's really annoying when everything becomes poetic,
when cleaning the kitchen becomes a metaphor for life,
when walking the dog becomes a metaphor for life,
when blowing your nose becomes
a metaphor for,
well maybe not life, probably relationships.

When does life become life, and living grand enough
in just the living? Washing dishes is just washing
dishes, and that's fine, because, after all
you need to eat off those dishes and an empty plate
doesn't have to be the symbol for world hunger
and a full plate the symbol of gluttony.

Let's just sit down, founder on
fried chicken, mashed potatoes oozing with gravy,
corn on the cob swimming in butter,
and clean up.

Troublesome Creek '93

She was only two and tired of socks
so she lobbed her shoes, one footless vessel
drifted sideways out of sight, the other caught
in the brambles which dipped their roots
far over the edges of the creek.

We lived in a hiccup of a town called Ary.
This was before the Diamond Coal Company
decapitated the Alleghenies, this was when
the mountain bloomers were full
and redbuds, dogwoods, skirted the valleys.

Now, the water settles, a cemetery of puddles
caught in between rock bed tombstones.
The blasting, at least, is over. It's quiet,
like a screaming child finally fallen
into a fitful sleep.

On that day, though, when I was still new
to my daughter and she to me,
we were pebble skipping and counting
the echoes of detonation, the thunder
of collapsing mountains against the softer ricochets

of wrinkling water, and the carcass of a deer
rolled by. A stop and go of hooves over
hindquarters, then antlers sloughed up the muck.
The brambles caught and held the pelt as bits
of flesh and fur floated off the hide.

A wood thrush trilled. I pulled my daughter away,
screaming. She wanted to stay, she wanted to help.
When I said the word "dead" to her for the first time,
I promised her bubbles, peanut butter and jelly,
purple dinosaurs.

Harper Lee

I will not hide behind my words, there has been enough of this.
There is a place where desire and thought are as real
and solid as a kitchen table.
I live here. If I were to speak to you, face to face, across this table,
I would say to you—you with the tree in your eye
(biblical reference) earth's a mote (another one) the crust
of sleep in God's eye and when we are done with words,
when they no longer need us, there will be giants to suck our bodies
like dust through their noses.

Come sun up.

Soldier on the front line, my brother
wakes in the West at 5 a.m.
because someone has to.
There will come a wobble, the stomach
will start to eat itself. Scientists aren't so sure,
but the Mayans say so. The earth will shimmer,
the ground around explode, temples in Yonaguni
will rise, the orders will come down

hold this ground, hold it, no matter
what comes over that horizon.

I will take the prayer beads from my neck
as the bullets are arranged in tally marks
my breath will fog white into the pitch
and I will say goodbye again and again.

Loom

Sunlight in the kiva,
        white shell, crystal
lightning. The crimson threads a horizon line
        as the peddles click-clack, clack-
click up and down, moving you
        no-where, where you will go, willingly
to await the arrival
        of sapphires in the threading,
of sunspots which thunderhead
        all along the fourth world.
See the stairway diamond into light
        there, at the ceiling?
Ni'hookaa Diyan Diné. Escalante ancestor.
        Oh voiceless one, oh Weaver
Woman—stagger the wind,
        steal our names from thunder
toss them in a moon puddle
        to soak past dawn,
then when the sun is high
        and red-faced, give breath to the color of birth
so we will not forget
        our cave, your sky.

Make Believe

In the morning I will get up

    You told me to just pretend you never called.

I will take a bath, wash my hair, brush my teeth and get dressed.

    To convince myself

I will go to the kitchen

    we never spoke, to trick my memory into thinking of a movie, a song

I will turn on the lights and open the fridge

    because the mind can make itself believe anything

I will look and look and keep looking.

    then the bullet to your brain wouldn't matter, just pretend

I will not think about that one morning you never made me breakfast

    I never knew you, pretend we never spoke, you've moved on

never brought me scrambled eggs and cheese in bed.

    I've moved on.

I will say that if it wasn't for Sundays, real butter, pancakes and maple syrup

    I would—I know I would.

Paper Philosophy

Split wings, wet chrysalis, sun-dried flight.
"We are at the point of crisis…it is paper which can lead us out."
It was only an earthquake.

(origins: Ts'ai Lun A.D. 105) Silk, hemp, recycled rags and fishnets.
Gutenberg's sheepskin. Illuminations in the Book of Hours.

It was only a hundred years ago we started looking towards the trees.

(The age of Mold and Deckle 1900's to the present day.)
Blue shells, a puzzle, scattered in the nests. One feather, brown and spotted.

It is good to listen to ghosts when they whisper, fill your mouth with sounds.
They'll talk all night long if you don't.

The process starts with clouds, no change, same pattern
repeating in the same form,
over and over since the first volcanic eruption, earth, straw
sucking water stem, root hairs,
sap goes through the vessels to branches. (Not like arms)

"If you are a poet you will clearly see the cloud in this paper."[1]
I know where monarchs go mom, but where do the birds fly?

Chickadee flute blowing at a lipstick sky.

Do they sing because they are happy?

It is only a turning tsunami which furls
in the corner a web,

What is the name of this leaf? What tree did it fall from?

Innocence, the rush of waves,
where have all the small spaces gone?

---

1 from *Heart of Understanding* by Thich Nhat Hanh

How Many Poets Does it Take to Change a Light-bulb?

Behold!

The Light-Bulb, glowy thing, filament of spiral flame! Oh,
Bulb of Light, Light bulbing bud, oh bud of fire, changing,
the screw, circular motion of hand, lefty loosy, righty tighty,
screw the screwing screws, screwed.

Illuminate! Ruminate! Postulate! What was lighted of the Bulb
Is light, where does the light go when the room is not light, what light
Through yonder winder breaks, why it is the east and who am I? Who
are you?

Wait—where does this go again?

Concrete

She takes the chalk and draws a mancala
on the sidewalk. Broken terracotta pots
become cinnamon-colored stones,
gravel from the road completes the game.

Oh, daughter, shattered vessels
are so often discarded, seldom saved,
but the sweetness of this wisdom reforms me
and nothing is lost. Nothing is lost.

A Question About What's Essential

The 40-watt mini-moon to kill the dark
and the closet door kept closed so the house
and the children can sleep. The smell
of your husband on the shirt you tuck yourself
into while he's away, the midnight invasion
of a 5-year-old who tells you to scoot over,
sing him "the valley so low" the monsters
don't like that song. The voice of your 14-
year-old daughter on stage for the last time
singing "don't try to fix me I'm not broken,
I'm still here, don't cry." Two days after
her best friend killed himself, tell me,
what reason is there for any of this?

Opus 40

after Dara Weir

You've got to be (seven kinds of) stupid
to open (a door) and hit yourself (in the head)

(may as well) (own it)

The glass is wavy. (Old glass) (fishbowl)

(mental images) (do not) (really exist)
So (take me) (literally)

How long before (you son of a bitch)
that sucker punch stops (pinching) (my lungs)

each time I think of you. You said:
(your skin is so soft)
that's all. (I want

to forget) fall in (the quarry of)
granite (move) (the stone
sculptures) (over) bury me (here)

Tankas to Float Down the River for Mara's 40th Birthday

What lingers among
the branches where the blooming
clouds sigh, life, oh life.
Flowering rain, dew, trees
stalking the dawn, ends this dream.

A river mouths sounds,
is spitting up pebbles along
sand-banks, eroded
beds of tree roots keep what washes
in the rain. Why this language. Is.

If we were granted
some magic or enough grace
to bid the clouds, speak,
they'd whisper: loam and soil, rock
and the sway of earth, not sky.

City on the Sea

The face decays, sinking daily, while the tourists spend
more than they should for a memory of the current
pushing the gondolas through thin canals. The wake belts
the buildings. Ezra Pound, for too long, followed this tide
and now, in this archipelago, this water of un-rested flow,
he finally rests. But for twelve years, twelve! To protect

his mind from reminding him, St. Elizabeth was supposed to protect
what remained of his mind, and yet the days he was to spend
the days, the days reminded him too much of Venice. The flow
of ancient arts, what songs they sung, and a moon-hung current.
Forget the moon, and Pound too. There's nothing to tide
the decay of facades, though with words we surge, we belt

we bellow, and we place ourselves outside, or in the sky, to un-belt
Orion's sword and claim the hunter's bow our own, and vow to protect
what we call beauty—say it. Love. To what else are we tied?
Salt and sand and city and sea and flesh and words we waste and spend
our breath counting what comes next and what goes in the currents.
Nothing stays, we know this. We know it. But still the flow

repeats itself just enough. Recede, diminish, returning again to flow
along that canal in Venice, where a gondolier without his song, belts
and bellows over the price of a memory, this tourist trap—currency
tendered. I would not name this place, or rather I would protect
the name, leave it alone, so those tourists can have their moment, spend
their time haggling. But you know this place, beyond tides

where the mermaids go to wait upon the rocks, and the tide
will come and all a manner of life also, with that flow.
God damn it, Ezra, why'd you leave Idaho? Why did you spend
more than you had? Did you have to unhook your belt
that day, couldn't you have just tried a little harder to protect
your mind from Venice? Damn the man-made currents.

Oh let me be, Orion. No—let me be Orion. Riding the current
of the night sky, the movement of stars is fixed but we move, the tide
moves against us and what words we gather to protect
whatever buildings remain and still float above the flow.
You can talk to the sea. Speak now, to spite the sewage, the un-belted
asses shitting word tsunamis into the sea, rotten stomachs spent.

The Doll Head Stories

1.   She cried when he played wishbone with the plastic legs, but when he shoved lightning bugs in the decapitated head, she laughed. The synthetic skull now an enchanted cranium that she put next to her bed and used for a night light; the face flushed with a more kindred glow.
2.   The baby had a sad face. One lash-less eye clicked sleepily, the other stayed closed. It made an odd gurgle which sounded more like a morose cow. It had no hair or eyebrows. Little sis knew the remedy, a black marker. Big sis was not happy, targeted her victim carefully. Beneath Raggedy Anne's triangle nose she drew a Hitler moustache. They never forgave each other.
3.   The infinite injustices done to Barbie. So many scalped by neighbor boys, who were overly fond of duct tape and scissors. Those were the real deal, not like the Walgreen fakes, the ones with those ridiculous unbendable knees and shoes that always fell off their feet.
4.   Holes where hair should be. Holes where there once were eyes. A plaster hand for a body, a thumb for the right arm. This is the empty socket, the empty mousetrap, the rotting cheese on the empty mousetrap, the delicate eyebrows penciled above that which the mouse crawls through. Not the mouse.
5.   Where is that damn mouse? Who gives a shit about a mouse anyway? I guess we'll just animate it. Cut to scene. Fade out. Won't it be funny? Won't we laugh? Nothing to an empty but crawling through it. The head of a doll balanced on fingers, the discarded is a white sculpture of a hand. The discarded is art.
6.   So doll baby is all in and of the thing crawling, the crawling through the empty, the vacant. Baby doll, baby doll doll baby oh baby do, oh do. Oh do doll babies get kept, get to keep the just enough, the plaster, the hand, the finger, the thumb?
7.   New arrival, re-gifted from my father-in-law—a porcelain Native American doll, left hand and left leg shattered. Thought it was the corpse of a child one morning when I woke up, walked into the living room and saw the fringed dress covering its face.

At the Outline of Night

Why did you come here
to haunt this song?
You faded from the sway of the earth
into, still, some echo, some blur on the horizon.
I can feel your emptiness
on my skin.

Don't, stay. Don't go.
Dawn, I refuse you, let the multitude of days be
one night.

I take it back.

Not the night you called,
a gun at your temple.

I take it back.

Here—a sunset, we are climbing
a rusted water tower, unremarkable clouds
above us, a dove singing down the sun. The light
is overcome as acorns succumb to gravity,
the quiet
is toppled by their falling,

into a fire of leaves, paper-thin, crisp
scent of autumn
flickers against the ever-growing dark
and my brown hair and your eyes—
copper? topaz? still warm.

Treading Consciousness

It's working on the hull with a fresh coat of paint
when the sails are scraps, a tattered cabin
quilt patchwork of questionable fabric
with water sloshing in the gut
and the bow of the ship
going under

or worrying
about the wires in the walls of a house
and running from room to room to check
all the receptacles while the house teeter-totters
on the lip of a volcano and magma sputters
across the front porch.

Don't say the moon
is anything but a battered vessel,
or a glorified rock. Don't let the cold, hard footprints
of light, breaking light, which bleeds into
darkening skies,
overthrow you.

Whence Came Thou—Watermelon

Do you have to be so pop-tarty, sprouting unplanned, unplanted
among my mums and dianthus?
I knew you were no weed, but what confection or vine you were
a mystery as full and bloated as a tick, now the size of a softball
resting all striped and green in the mulch.
Would it be a sin to separate you from your environment,
once foreign now home?

My hand stalls at the plucking to wonder if it is better
to be left to rot, join the earth and become the eternal dirt,
evolving, the way dirt does, or if with a bit of salt
to be tasted, preserved in me, some memory of fruit.

I don't know the answer, so I wait to see what,
when left to yourself, your pulp may feed.

Frames, unhinged

I am certain the ghosts
are reading the books in my library
so I leave one open in the kitchen
each night and I tell my husband
it is because I like to cook and read at the same time.

Then I give him the "I dare you to say I'm crazy" look.
Hopefully they (the ghosts) will pardon
the BBQ thumbprints.
But I think, after I've gone off to bed, they swirl
around my kitchen, considering the pages only briefly
before moving on to the topic of meatloaf
and potatoes all the while wishing
that they had thumbs.

At 12:30 the golliwogs come and chase them
around the houses across the world. Last night
I woke up at 3 a.m. for the third time this week.
My fingers intertwined beneath my chin as if posed
in prayer.

I wonder if this is the hour time condenses, like frost (not dew)
on the inside of a car window that you forgot to roll up, or
maybe it just gathers all together beneath the dark,
in swift currents because something keeps swimming
inside my skin and wakes me, makes me believe
the dead want to pray, but can't, they have no lips
or thumbs.

Time to Go (a ballad)

Under the rocky mountain's shoulder
A century plant's in bloom
In a place they call rainshadow
The desert's dusty tomb.

Joshua trees eat all our graves
And we dance in frames of fire
She knows our name is Mojave now
So she whispers, Liar, liar.

Oh Kodachromes, oh kodachromes,
Escalante's red sandstones
Dries the bones, dries the bones.

This place was never paradise
So why do you abide?
He's six feet under the sandstone now,
Why stay so long at his side?

Your mother lives at Pipe Springs
She's still among those living
She waits for you to come to her,
Find her and be forgiven.

Oh Kodachromes, oh kodachromes
Escalante's red sandstones
Dries the bones, dries the bones.

I must find my grandmother
There is something that I know
The blooming plant marks the place
Her grave was lost long ago.

Three taps there is outside the door
Three taps—long-limbed moon stalker,
Three taps she sings her dying song,
Sings to the light walker.

No one is there outside the door.
No one inside worth saving.
So who is coming back for you,
No one but sagebrush waving.

Oh Kodachromes, oh kodachromes
Escalante's red sandstones
Dried the bones, dried the bones.

Free Falls

Residue of hushing
last rights of buttercups and bleached
whale bones with living seaweed
stuffed in the holes of the house
the walls cackle, forget the skin
and moan of tides.

Twice-shattered teeth,
note to self sketched on the flesh
of an esophagus trilling with elegies
wonder, the whys, open throat
cough, swallow,
look the other way.

Henna ink along each finger
a long marriage in Pateli's palm,
and around each wrist
vines spiral entwine
a checkerboard below her thumb.

Again, the cobwebs,
the long dark dreams
of sleeping spiders
of men with no sight
who see through the slits
in the palms of their hands.

In a swamp, the alligator claims an arm.
Cumberland would reconcile
the loss. It falls just enough to flow
across turtle sentinels and fool moon's
night, some see the moonbow.

Lalla Ded sang without complaint
though her bowl of rice
was filled so often with rocks
her tongue kept the taste of pebbles.
Scotch taped clock on the bookshelf,
minus second, useless bookends, correct
time found here if nowhere else.

No broken marble statues or finger-
touching god etched or brushed
in painted dance, a dream, a crack
in the Sistine chapel ceiling
counts down the universe
from ten to one.

There's the first scribes vice,
vellum, the skin scraped at each mistake
and catchwords at the folio gatherings.
Before this, China's silk
and hemp and rags.

Sacred drums, turtle rattles, gone,
buildings and songs abandoned
to the monuments of sleeping,
but the dead know stone
and prefer dim-lit porches where cobwebs
at least sigh a little as they pass through.

Cosmic Constructions

The moon's romance was wasted
on the dust of the first moonwalker's feet.
Science is its own religion. What the hell
is anti-matter anyway? Likely the origins
of all things polyester.

What happens when we are brave
or stupid enough to measure lightning
with a ruler? Oh Vitruvius.
De architectura. Consider
the ruined columns of the temple.
It's not easy to be as incorruptible
as stone.

Galileo got it wrong.
Galileo, who in the Dialog of the Ebb
and Flow of the Sea,
called out the moon for folly,
became Galileo, the man in chains.
No one would hear. No one would see.
His terrestrial telescope, broken.

Does revelation have a surface
or a center? Look elsewhere.
Look through.

Tonight, the sky is missing a moon.
Orion inclines over the earth,
his belt buckle rides the horizon.

The Cowboy's Rain-dance

I wished you would have kicked the sun
across the horizon with those stupid cowboy boots,
or at least tipped your hat when you flipped God the bird.

Your diety was Clint Eastwood whose six shooter was pointed
at your head at all times, from your world you brought back proof:

the butt of a cigarette, a broken bit of glass shaped like a dove.
I watched you struggle to be free from those boots, drunk
in the storm, yelling at God: "You shitter, all you do is shit!"

And no reply but mine. "There's no one out there, dad,
please come in out of the storm."

So

you say I need to see a shrink
again 'cause
      I'm singin'
rounds
around the garbage—

    Oh say can you see
    by the dawn's early light?

as I take out the trash
with proudly hailed screams,
confessions, crumpled paper
cup accusations
at twilight's last gleaming.

And the rocket's red glare
(Does this poem still exist if no one reads it?)
the bombs bursting in air
gave proof through the broken
rubber, semen, waste
and coffee grounds. Doesn't it?

Doesn't just a spoonful of sugar
make the medicine go down,
medicine
go down. And all the smart bombs
and all the footless children
get together, make Humpty
Dumpty omelets.

Does that star-
spangled
      banner yet wave?

Eggshells, eggshells, eggshells,
got to break a few—y'know?

Oh say—

I'm sorry.
I know I'm not making much sense
to you, stumpy—God.
I hate you, and your shoes.
(does air still exist if no one breathes it)
Let's be ironic. Let's bury the vampires alive
so they'll die of hunger.
Let's make sure every poem has a cloud and sky,
a fucking you
a fucking I.

Forward this message home if you will.
Send lightning.

The Imp of the Perverse (revisited)

Tonight, it could all be a funny joke
and you'd laugh too
if not for the elephant sitting on your chest.
Not a crush like the apocalypse,
the sun finally exploding,
chunks of sky falling in.

Windows dripping down the walls.
Worlds, melting, merging,
liquid/solid.

This night will not be
a refreshing sip of salvation.

Best try to manage it in shapes,
the shell of the smooth,
your shadow in a frame.

~~~
The sheets say whisper
but senselessly so
one-dimensional here.  Do you know
it doesn't matter, or do you turn
and tumble, twisted and tangled
in the sky?

~~~
Always the conclusion of glass
cooled into a solid or molten
the substance is the same. Knock, Knock.
Who's there?
Fucking ravens. A brass knob turns
as serpents sip tea and discuss curses.

Inside your breath smudges
against the stubborn and hard.
Proof of life, but never enough.
Your shoulders are hot
because you've been sick all day.

Still you must work
press a finger to the glass
watch the warmth of your imprint fog.

Somewhere hydrogen fuses with oxygen.
Somewhere it falls, fades, falls again.

Star City Coffin Club

for Andrew and Gary

The brakes on the train sing   in the distance
     needle to bone   tattooed, needle down to bone, ink skips
but it won't stop, not here,   not anymore.
     slips under the skin, piercing,   no, not piercing, etching
We don't know what to name this   so we say inertia   (this text)
     oh living vellum don't say it hurts,
when stars are too many and   numbers won't do.
     just hold it together, draw invisible faces on the window
breaking and entering is just a game of X's and O's,
     write poetry with your finger on the wall.
movement happens, your life is a sentence punctuated
     even in your solitude and stillness when you settle
in the paragraph of the house, the bedroom, the bed,
     like a pebble sinking, remember, count to sixty (one minute)
what you planted in a plastic cup when you were five.
     Count to sixty again (two minutes).
This is why the children cut themselves,
     When the teacher explained how all things deepen or rise
to annunciate the flesh,
     in their own time, and always in this what is left
a cummerbund and pillows?
     This is why they burn the houses down
The peace, the dust in the coffin, the neon glow over the city,
     becomes a testimony   a sacred text
this is why he took a rope and hung himself.
     the sharp white shred a corner of charred paper
         all that's left in an ash-pile underneath the window
            of his room.

The Year of the Stink Bug

The year the stink bugs came
all the ladybugs disappeared;
I think they ate them, or at least
that's what I was told.

The year the stink bugs came
the rainbows developed a narrative
arc, where the velocity of time
was instantaneous and infinite.

But how can this be? To a stink bug
time is only ever a mud puddle.
The year the stink bugs came
they took over the bank and I got a job.

It was the year I wasn't home,
the year I started counting stop-lights
between here and there. The year
of stink bugs became

The year of frozen lasagna, the year
of diminished minutes, of not enough
time to cook fresh broccoli. If the rainbow
really did become a narrative arc

Who would be telling this story?
How long would it last?
(Pssst. The answer is not Science
Nor infinite.)

The year the stink bugs came
we wrecked two cars in one month,
and many stink bugs died, and many did not.
I'm sure this was their fault.

Did you know if you run over a stink bug
It will not die? There was once a year
of the ladybug. There was. The year
the mud puddles took on the rainbows

and won eternal glory, the shallowness
was instantaneous. The velocity of a mud puddle
is instantaneous. (Sometimes, infinite
as a pothole.) When hit by a car, that is.

The mud became infinite. Dirt does not decay,
you know, dirt only becomes more dirt-ish.
The infinite mud, oh the infinite mud there
was, as ever, no point to all of this.

I think that God wears shoes

probably oxfords with that funny tassel, or red high heels,
or black military boots.
I hear he wears a purple turtleneck, walks asphalt roads and hops along
double yellow lines. But I don't think it matters, he's blind, of course,
but some say they've seen him leap over the left-hand lane
dodging cars by sound.
And because I believe in a God who wears Shoes, or
because I believe in the God-shoe,
I also believe I can explode at any moment, torched with a click-flick
of his pointer finger bic.

But I'd venture he's done roasting wishbones
of sacrificial chickens over lava pits. Done with the damning of nasty
grannies, done with peering
in windows. Sacrifices still on an altar of simplicity but
when the lightning smell crackles the air it has its own sacred noise
and it is no more than the sound of bare feet splashing in a puddle.

What sometimes you find

when you look in the garbage

"Tres Personjas" a widow's tossed painting.
Tamayo of Zapotec descent. Lost Oaxaca in purple fins,
red breasts, square head, outlines in barest of blues.
Ladders up, ladders down, it all started off stolen
anyway. Hooks in the sky, a door, a leg, an arm, a baby,

not porcelain, not immune to the sound of breaking glass.
Texture, measuring tape, divining lines, see-through circles
around the invisible, eggshells, broken coffee cup,
perspective.

Underneath it all a cell rings
and rings, and rings

Freak Show 4: Gone Rogue

1916

No, it's not because of ivory and no poachers did the deed.
Mighty Mary swung while the children cheered:
"Kill the elephant, Kill the elephant!" It was because she bent
to eat a watermelon rind and her trainer, a man named Red,
gouged her ear. So she stepped on his head.

1903

There's no excuse for Topsy either. Sure, they fed her
a lit cigarette a time or two, but what right did she have
to crush a man's chest? Thomas Edison took care of her.
Filmed it even: "The Electrocution of an Elephant."
Famous footage, certainly.

1994

Okay, perhaps Tyke was just tired, had enough of chairs, pulling ropes
little pricks poking all the time. He took down three men
before 86 bullets took him down. He fell, one last rumbling roar
died low in his throat.

Now

Halfway across the world in Africa, the sound of chains
pounding around their heated skulls, tuskless elephants
flick their ears and trample a village without cause.

Ice Storm

The power was out in three states. The candle
sputtered and died in a wickless wax puddle
on the dresser. What light there was came from outside.

We all crowded together. I clung to what inches
of mattress I could. There was a leg over my neck
and someone else's knee in my back. The baby

latched on to my breast and would not be moved.
Unmindful of the sound of sleet belting the house,
they snored, quiet gusts of breath rose, evaporated

in the air. I waited—for sleep, or for light,
or for my husband who was not here,
who was somewhere out there, climbing poles.

Nothing came, not even dawn. It seemed
the day could not quite gather itself. The children
did not know when to wake up so they slumbered

on and on, until the sound of groaning boughs.
The house shuddered. I rushed to a window.
They followed, hands clutched whatever part of me

they could reach, stuck their noses so close
their breath misted the glass. Outside—
the oak split in two. The whole world crystallized.

Even the gravel driveway turned prism, the house
a crystal cocoon, and just inches from my front door,
the ruin of a tree.

For no good reason, I worried about the sparrows.

My Children Picked the Berries from the Hollytree

They saved the rabbit from the creepy cat,
Then brought it home in hopes that I might tend
The wounds, and help it heal. Though I knew that

A promise would not change how this could end.
It was too small, so they chose a strong name
A name which would repair, a name to mend

The broken bones, and heal what would be lame.
It seemed to work at first. Leonidas,
Destined to be the King of Rabbits, fame

Of his miraculous life, his near miss
With death, would spread to all of the warrens!
Each night they sent him to sleep with a kiss,

Then said a prayer that he might hop again.
And though we loved the best we could, one day
We found him cold and still, and then—and then

The Bookbinding Lesson

> "The book as a physical object is an exploration...Compilation can never yield a book. A sense of format is glimpsed through introspection."
> —Keith A. Smith, *Non-adhesive Binding, Books without Glue or Paste*

Paper has a memory,
she said. I remember.

Use the bone folder to smooth the spine
and leave a space for the gutters.

Same old, cold November, down Hawthorne Street
on the way to school I bite the ends
off the black icicles hanging from my hair.

Be careful with the bodkin,
don't stab through the backbone.

When your feet have followed the same sidewalk
a thousand times, there is nothing complicated about walking,
even in a flurry, even when the ice-coated path hardens and cracks.

Leave no fingerprint in the folios. Use a Weaver's knot
to attach new thread to the old.

Snow saturates my worn-out sneakers.
I leave marks the shape of oblong boats behind me.
I try to make my steps more tender.

Langsten and Kettenstitch. Mind your sewing stations,
don't get sloppy with the knots.

Paper has a memory. I remember. She said.

When the tree is gone the pulp is pressed
and the paper bleached. There is, at least, this.

What we carry home

There was a baby on my hip when the man in the suit, with a briefcase and a cell-phone stuck to the side of his head, cut in front of me. Return trip after a funeral, I wore sunglasses to hide my eyes, and I had no fire left and because he knew he could, he did, and I didn't even flare, not a flicker, but my mother, who was watching, came over and took my place in line. She said nothing to me or him, just stood there, arms folded, until it was time for my baggage to be checked. I sat on my suitcase and cried. Tried to stop but couldn't. On the airplane I sat next to a man with two small daughters. The man wore faded jeans with ripped-out knees and work boots. The girls looked to be about four and eight and were talking, talking, talking, their father to death, literally, it seemed. He was too skinny, looked like he hadn't shaved or slept in a week. They bounced all over the place. He sat with one hand covering his face. They had no mother. Or at least, none that cared. I could tell by the ponytails. It was obvious that a man's hands had made the attempt. A father always leaves the rubber band too loose. A good father, anyway, is afraid of pulling hair, afraid of hurting, and the end result is always a mess. A mother, on the other hand, with years of experience pulling her own hair high and tight, will center a ponytail, choking off any strays.

I was nursing the baby and the girls started to ask me questions. The man looked over at me, embarrassed, apologizing. I smiled and explained I had five kids at home and was used to it. Quietly so his daughters couldn't hear him he whispered: "Their mother doesn't want them anymore. Told me to come and get them. She's not been nice to them."

One sat near me, pressed herself as close to me as she could and leaned her head on my shoulder. No wonder. The other pushed herself past the baby on my lap and talked the whole ride home. No wonder. The father fell asleep and didn't move until the plane touched down. He apologized again and when he said, "I'm sorry if they bothered you, but thank you." He meant it, and when I said "Not at all, they are precious." I meant it, too. Those were the last words I spoke to him before he walked away, the older girl holding on by his shirt with one hand while with the other she clutched her little sister's fingers. The little one was looking back at me, dragging her feet, but eventually she stuck her thumb in her mouth and seemed resigned to follow. I watched until a tunnel filled with people swallowed them, until my own child started to cry and needed my attention. At my breast, after he had calmed, he stared at me hard for a long time. Then he raised his chubby fingers and mopped the tears from my face. I did not feel blessed. He poked both my eyes and giggled as he gave my hair a yank, but something lifted from me then and left me light.

Surprise Epilogue at Dawn

This morning's earth is an obvious round.
You can tell by the sound. The sky is bent;
the dent of stratospheric clouds feather
frozen, refuse to budge. Sliver of moon
lasts 'till noon then dissolves to blue
as all things do which ring around the sun.
Heaven always leaps between dawn and dusk,
not so dappled today. Still, say what
you will, a man just wants to make his family
happy. What else is true but work?
A gallon of milk, a loaf of bread, children
asking questions. See? She said love, he said.
If he can't have this he, himself, dissolves.

Lunar Navigator

My child, my son, his body
embraces his age awkwardly, thirteen,
he's memorized maps of the moon,
from the light of the Northwestern Limb
to the shadows of the Crater Grimaldi and he dreams
of a reality without gravity. Feathers and stones.

Stones and feathers. He knows how to calculate
his weight on Mars. He can tell you how many light years
to the spiral galaxy; he can explain why a rock
and a penny drop to earth with the same velocity,
but he cannot find his face, because he can't find a hand
to push the hair from his own forehead,
look the girl he likes in the eye and smile.

Luminosity: Radiant energy and other forms

Broken.

Through your kitchen window a universe of motes, dust
rides currents of light, settles down into the cracks on the floor.
You see a blinking, maybe it's a signal from somewhere.
You can take that warmth, bank on it, reach for it
hands orbiting, fingers spiral to catch—
nothing. There is only the pattern
of lines in an empty palm, those etchings
identified you before you knew yourself.

Electric.

Wires run like vessels in the body of your home
to outlets. Faith would say it is a simple thing,
on or off. (But there is always voltage running through).

Hidden.

Between the shadow and the shadow caster there is a world
trapped under the same bushel which covers you, and when you are ripe
for sleep, when you breathe down deep to the bottom of your lungs
there will be that lingering sweet scent of harvest.
Crisp-apple sugar maple leaf.

Borrowed.

You are dreaming. That smell is only the night. Can I mention Autumn
one more time?
Divining lines? Reflections are a child's joy, the first taste of rain and
puddle's stomped,
mud between toes. Some comet that's been gone so long its name has
been forgotten.

Last time we sat around the campfire watching the flames and
debating currents:
electric, rivers, wind, how dark and cold the air sung through us,
but when you glanced up at me, the fire burned away that song.

Dad's Tomatoes

There are three things I will never forget about my father.

He wore cowboy boots. When he came home from work he'd fall to the chair, lift them in the air, "heel then toe," he'd always say. I'd yank them off, land on my butt, then put them back on, wading around the room in his laughter.

He used to kick holes in doors. Sometimes it seemed he wanted to break himself, beating his boots against the wood, but always the doors broke first so that solid thing inside him stayed hard and whole. Other times he'd just spill, like red kool-aid on the carpet. The worst times he oozed like hot tar on a tin roof.

He played guitar and sang The Green Green Grass of Home, Proud Mary, and Tie A Yellow Ribbon 'Round the Old Oak Tree...if you still love me. We danced on the couch and chairs and no one cared.

There are three things I had forgotten about my father.

He used to talk to people who weren't there. Or maybe they were, but I never saw them.

He came to my high-school graduation dressed in a mushroom colored 70's suit wearing a shirt my mom had made for him ten years before. The last remnant of fifteen years of marriage. He was there, I didn't say hello. Then he was gone.

He told me once, "God is an asshole. He sits in heaven shitting all over us, laughing. We're here to suffer. That's it." All I could think to say was, "No. That's not true," and hug him as he wept in my lap because my mom would not take him back.

There are three things I wish I could forget about my father.

I used to dream about him being chased and eaten by wolves, so I could not hate him. Even though I still remember how he screamed at my sister when the car wouldn't start. Even though I still remember my little brother waiting all day on the couch. Dad said he would come. Grandma always told me I was his favorite. That didn't make me happy.

He died, alone, forgotten for three days or more in the filth of a hole he called home. They had to cremate him, there wasn't enough left to bury. We gathered wildflowers, tall seed grass, and spread his ashes near the Cougar Mountain cascades, in the bend of the Boise river, underneath an old bridge, spreading daisies, buttercups, indian paintbrush, milkweed, and queen anne's lace to follow him along the flow. A father and his daughter sat on an outcrop fishing. I watched as he helped her throw out a line.

He was there, then he was gone, and I didn't say good-bye. Near the rat's nest of his home all he left in this world was a garden: green peppers, corn, squash, and tomatoes heavy and ripe as the sun as it drops down the V of Cougar mountain; not a weed between the rows.

Graveyard

Across heaven's backbone
they tell me
this yoke will be light.
Light. A precipitation
of grace, the cloud
in the drinking glass.

Rain.
is. Or is not. Resurrection's
waterway, father's ashes
cloud the river.
Cinder to seepage.

The maggots feasted
at least four days
before his body was found.
Marble eyes make
for a heavy mind.
The river will not rest.

Say there is a kindness in death.
Tell me of dignity.
What is dead
is dead. No tombstone
but pebbles.

What else is there to offer here
but gutted wildflowers?
Milkweed thistle
parachutes
as if to escape.

Indian paintbrush
caught in the shallows,
dad in the belly of a trout
or in the silt underneath
an algae coated rock.
Queen anne's lace
and goldenrod
spin and spin
petal to stem
stem and petal.

Look up

Into the whorl, into the star-fed sea

Shell of an ear, a colossal cochlea,

Home of the bell-bones

Which tremble in weightlessness.

Out there

The sun sounds like a sandstorm,

Saturn's rings crackle

And beyond the static God

Runs a thumb along the lip of the universe

As if tuning a water glass.

Gifts of Faith (Without Conviction)

To move a mountain, my mother sends me chocolates
but the box is filled with rocks, rose quartz,
eggshell agates, creamy orange jasper, and dark
breccias drizzled with white limestone.

I take the weight of bloodstone in my hand.
I want to sink my teeth into its smooth green pulse.

My sister always sends dragonflies. This time though,
a wind-chime, eagle feather, and paper.

I imagine you looking over a silver wing, through glass
a passenger in each airplane that crosses my sight,
the architect of kanji and everything else I can't read,
the rain perfumed by oceans.

Listen, this path is mercurial.
X marks the spot in the ozone where I hope you are
each time, but there is only a glint of metal, a banquet
of flames forming exhausted clouds.

So here I am again, with a stomach full of pebbles,
a water-strider sent to sky walk, sinking fast.

Energy Efficient

She washed the stones in moonlight
gathered our bodies
a feather and dream catcher
recycled star-dust and a flash-light.
Seasons of the universe—my sons.

Two silver and jade necklaces,
material of galaxies, a hoodie that says,
"Arizona," sterling and opal earrings,
circuits of dawn, my daughters.

She kept watch all through the night
till dusk was full of shining conduits,
umbilical fire and ash from whence
came the first born

Born on a Blue Day (Daniel Tammet)

To adopt chaos a mind might recite π for hours.

Two is yellow, six a void, five a clap of thunder,

The Rosetta Stone

profound talent and profound disability are divided by a thin line.

Not even an eyelash.

Each hair on the human head has a number, the sparrow
falls without counting. Intelligence is not a gift,

it is a cracker-jack prize, a wash-off tattoo,
a plastic compass, the candy coating on the popcorn,
or likely just the nuts which settle to the bottom
during shipping

1. *What is a baby goldfish called?*
2. *Where do iatrophobes fear to go?*
3. *When is a nightshade a vegetable?*
4. *'Hands' are a part of which religion?*
5. *In what sport do you throw stones at houses?*
6. *What is the collective noun for collective nouns?*

Wisdom, on the other hand, is a wonderful peculiar
pebble.

Aiken's Still Makin' Music

Oh spark on star-fingered shimmy shine man.
Combusting blue, ice comet, spaghetti bangs man.

Play that ladle ladle. Dance the solar system hoe down.
Never mind a pressing eclipse, never mind the night

light, silly Light-Bright smiling orbit face in heaven.
Maybe your just a rabbit thumpin' up a storm

on the moon's tranquil waterless seas. Winken, Blinken
and Nod say so, and also China. But not me, I still believe

in your meatball ears. I see your face pressed like a penny,
or a relief of one, in that reflection. Is that really you up there?

Must have been some sun casted line long, long ago
slipped slided you away, into a ripple, into a flair.

Freak Show 5: There have been dancing plagues before.

1518, Frau Troffea took to the street in Strasbourg
while sodden in the pulse of some silent swishing,
her mind clattered with the rush of harmonies
beyond the range of normal hearing. The disease
spread, like the smell of bacon or a grease fire.

Now if hailstorms or ergot-laced bread
Caused the mass dancing, the toe tapping
shuffle-suffering population to expire
in heat stroke or exhaustion, not one person knows.
But that old tail-twitcher—he takes the credit.

Preservation

My daughters watch me often,
even when I sleep they creep in.
I feel their gaze, a breath of feathers
on my face.

The only want my eyes.

My sons press against me,
bury their head in my chest
but they do not want me to hold on,
just my fingers, brief against their scalp.

They only want my scent.

There have been men in my life
who've pushed sound in my head.

They wanted my ears, not my lips
or tongue.

Each day I want less and less.
I'll keep my bones to myself.

Today, even though it is winter
I've found a dogwood blossom on the ground,
antiqued lace. I touch it
to my lips, the fragrance gone, falling apart
in my hands I'll save it in my dictionary

and someday, when the children have grown,
when I'm gone maybe they'll come across this too,
a simple love note, a faded heirloom on a page.

Attrition

Witness the hoo doos of the canyon lands or the hollow
spaces below the rainbow arches and you'll know
the wind and its echo.
Mountains are measured into sand, and sand
doesn't remember its genesis
even though when melted into glass
there is always a slope
coldly reflected.

Down in the mine the light hollows out the darkness
only enough for the imagination to consider
the weight of soil on the support beams.
There are no diamonds here. Nothing shines
but seepage, when you, soot-faced and darkened
lung, finally reach the surface again
the natural gloss of day is not radiant, but blinding.

Subtraction

The way any even amount of negatives
will always become a positive. Wait,
that doesn't add up. But it makes sense
in some equation:

minus sun, minus stars, minus moon, minus earth
times time.

There is more to reflect on waves, like how
they encircle one another, what moves them, us,
against, away from, the always, the momentum
the water in the wave,
the wave in the water.

Only the Air

> *Leave what's alive in the furrow, what's dead
> in yourself,
> for life does not move in the same way as a group
> of clouds*
> —Miguel de Unamuno

I'm smoking on my back porch and I see a hawk balancing on my neighbor's shed. In one claw he clutches a struggling chickadee, the other scratches the tar of the roof. The chickadee's mate swoops and trills, closer, closer. The hawk's gaze is nailed to the tall willow across the cul-de-sac.

This morning when I was looking for the cigarette stash in my bedroom closet I found tiny teeth marks on the butts and bits of tobacco and mouse droppings strewn in my shoes, like some strange after offering to their gods. I imagined them stuffing their furry cheeks and leaving spit marks on the inside of my walls

where two weeks ago some bird, probably a pigeon, flew in a crack and for four days I listened to the sound of its dying, its wings flapping like a runner on a treadmill. I couldn't sleep when the silence finally came.

Yesterday a monarch flew in my open door. It swirled around the ceiling fan, swooped with the air current and landed on my right shoulder. It stretched its wings wide like a slow yawn, or maybe more like a deep sigh of relief.

In winter I found a sparrow frozen in a tuft of dead goldenrods. I broke the hard ground, steam rising from my mouth, and buried it with a prayer because I read somewhere: "No sparrow falls without the Father." But I'm not sure if I believe that.

In spring I found a nest on my porch cupped in the geraniums. I watched five sparrow eggs hatch and spied on them until they grew into bloated furry balloons. One day, as I was sitting watching, one floated down to my toe cocked her head and chirped as if expecting I had something to offer her. I held myself frozen, held my breath until my vision blurred and my eyes watered, held it until my insides burned all that ice away and my lungs expanded like a life preserver and I didn't let it go until she flew away.

The next morning they were gone. Nothing left but a vacant nest, eggshells, a few bits of down cradled in between flower petals. When I saw them zooming from goldenrod to goldenrod down by the creek I felt like they were still mine. But where can I keep these things if not inside the walls of my cluttered mind, where the floor of this closet is just a memory littered with all of my own pathetic offerings to god.

I know the hunger of that hawk. I know why, and I know on what it would feed. Still, I want the chickadee to live. I will never really reach the truth of this though, because I've looked away to write you this, and now, where there was once a struggle, only waves of heat bend the air, rippling up from the black tar roof of the shed.

She fell asleep before the execution

Does water always burn this brightly?
She is wearing her wedding cake on her head,
cuts a piece for each guest as plates float,
clattering around her like boats with no anchor, and the centerpieces
are made of gigantic ice-frosted roses, edible
pink petals. In the corner the groom
downs mouthwash. When the guests sway forward to greet the bride,
she hands them each a plate and says,
"Here's your hat."

After Dreaming of Tornados

No one came to save us. We became effortlessly patient
in navigating channels of sound, waiting for the right echo,
the precise movement of words that would resurrect
the dead spots from the weight of the shattered structures,
but instead, we've only sunk deeper, yes, just another penny
dropped down a wishing well.

Should have wished harder. Should have shut up,
and let the after-silence speak for us, let the myth of ripples and reflections
bring us back to ourselves. But we were never there,
there was never anything to come home to, we were the penny
and never the water, the penny and not even the wish, not even
a reflected glimmer, some thin web of light breaking through,
just a piece of copper, corroding, settling into the darkness of our daily mud.

Let's pretend to believe in unicorns and pots of gold and butterflies
and tell this story over. She came to save you.
An angel whispered words into your ear and
your mind honeycombed with the light of heaven where God's
slow blinking sight never strays and where there is no wishing
only what is so and what is not so, here if there is a truth to find
in words, if there is something left worth saving in us or them,
let us be clear. Let us be real. Let us be true.

After a spring rain one day my children and I followed a rainbow
into a field of horses. This is not a metaphor; this was done
with full awareness of the color cast offs,
the prisms of illusions, what happens when you bend the sun.
We were not looking for leprechauns or four-leaf clovers,
but for the end. The rainbow bridged the sky and ended
in a budding maple. A colt dashed away, his hooves dragging
an ellipsis across the wet field, towards his mother.

I thought the bridge would disappear when we came to the tree,
but as we moved it moved, gliding further along the meadow to a fence.
I knew we'd never catch it but we chased it all the way
back behind Chestnut mountain, where we couldn't follow.

Mosaic

When I am old and as wrinkled as the napkin
next to my plate, I will sit and watch the dawn fall
through the window. I will not wish

this day is not the day it is
sprinkled like salt across my table, a tesserae
of light and shadow, it will be

September 11th, and it will be Groundhog's Day,
and it will be your birthday I have forgotten,
but instead of shadow, stone, and not the hiding

but the running away, or the running to,
how we always return to where we have been.
Here, the mercies of fear are gentle.

So, I will smooth the puckered fabric
across my lap, and forget
I'm making do.

Unearthed

A turtle turned over a rock and found words.
She ate them to become slow, wise
And living. She buried her eggs in the sand
She dug near the river and forgot

She ate them. To become slow, wise,
Carried like a pearl in her stomach.
She dug near the river and forgot
If she could sing she would sing a song of ash.

Carried like a pearl in her stomach,
A grain of sand would not cause less pain.
If she could sing. She would sing. A song of ash.
Cough up the pearl and spit it out.

A grain of sand would not. Causeless pain.
The hard shell cracks from inside out.
Cough up the pearl and spit it out
Or find a sundial and steal its shadow.

The hard shell cracks from inside out
The first thing to learn is how to breathe
Or find a sundial and steal its shadow
Then dance upside-down in the air.

The first thing to learn is how to breathe.
Think you are blue see you are green turned over,
Then dance. Upside-down in the air,
Drown in the sky and swim in the dirt to live.

Think. You are blue. See, you are green. Turned over,
A turtle, turned over a rock and found words.
Drowning the sky and swimming the dirt to live,
And living, she buried her eggs in the sand.

Axe in Hand (The Perpetually Present State of Poetry)

Hold the wood steady
as the blade swings.

Chop. The splinters fly, gather
the kindling. Ask for mercy,
or don't. Count your fingers

to teach that language.
May as well make a snake sign.

Do you accept the blindfold
or keep close watch on the skin
of your wrist?

The New York Quarterly Foundation, Inc.
New York, New York

Poetry Magazine

Since 1969

Edgy, fresh, groundbreaking, eclectic—voices from all walks of life.

Definitely NOT your mama's poetry magazine!

The *New York Quarterly* has been defining the term contemporary American poetry since its first craft interview with W. H. Auden.

Interviews • Essays • and of course, lots of poems.

www.nyquarterly.org

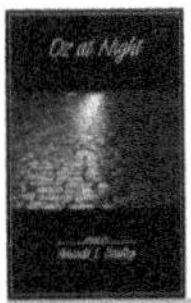

No contest! That's correct, NYQ Books are NO CONTEST to other small presses because we do not support ourselves through contests. Our books are carefully selected by invitation only, so you know that NYQ Books are produced with the same editorial integrity as the magazine that has brought you the most eclectic contemporary American poetry since 1969.

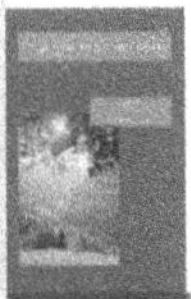

Books

nyqbooks.org

poetry at the edge™

www.ingramcontent.com/pod-product-compliance
Lightning Source LLC
LaVergne TN
LVHW041343080426
835512LV00006B/590